Litter Lady Leads

in a
Litter-filled
Land

Martha Goldner

To order additional copies of this book, contact:
Xlibris
844-714-8691
www.Xlibris.com
Orders@Xlibris.com

ISBN: 979-8-3694-1878-9 (sc)
ISBN: 979-8-3694-1877-2 (hc)
ISBN: 979-8-3694-1876-5 (e)

Library of Congress Control Number: 2024906249

Print information available on the last page

Rev. date: 08/22/2024

Meet Litter Lady.
She is old and caring.

Her cane has a pointy tip.
She picks up trash that other
people leave behind.

She can't help it.
Litter Lady likes to clean up.

She feeds us chocolate cookies from her big bag.

She is our friend.

She picks up gum wrappers from train seats.

She takes towels, tissues, and other trash off the bike trail.

At the beach, she takes sandy soda cans and suntan
bottles straight to the recycling container.

She finds homework sheets near the schoolyard.

She crumples old grocery lists she finds in
carts and puts them in her pocket.

She picks up plastic utensils and paper plates at the swim club.

Hot dog wrappers and catsup packets won't mess up seats at the ballpark if Litter Lady is at the game.

She can't help it.
Litter Lady likes to clean up.

At the movie theater, she grabs empty cups and popcorn buckets and puts them in the dumpster.

She cleans up sticks, glass, plastic, and other waste due to windstorms.

Litter Lady takes working appliances and clothing people don't want and gives them to the needy.

A vacuum is Litter Lady's treasured tool.

Lost coins don't
cause slipping
hazards when Litter
Lady is around. Her motto
is "Find a coin, pick it up;
all the day you'll have good luck!"

We saw Litter Lady on the ferry. She was
cleaning cigarette butts and candy wrappers.

How can Litter Lady enjoy herself when she is
always cleaning up other people's messes?

There is a lot of litter.

We saw Litter Lady at the bus stop.
She did not look well.

She didn't have cookies for us!

Can we help clean up?

Definitely, yes!

Will Litter Lady ever stop cleaning up trash?
Probably not.
She can't help it.

She has taught herself to make jewelry out of
aluminum can caps as well as gum wrappers!

She is a hero.

We pick up debris in the water.

Cleaning can be hard work, but we feel glad when we are finished.

Together we will make the world a brighter, happier place!

Printed in the United States
by Baker & Taylor Publisher Services